Women in the Workplace

WAGES, RESPECT, AND EQUAL RIGHTS

A YOUNG WOMAN'S GUIDE TO CONTEMPORARY ISSUES™

Women in the Workplace

WAGES, RESPECT, AND EQUAL RIGHTS

JERI FREEDMAN

ROSEN
PUBLISHING®

New York

Published in 2010 by The Rosen Publishing Group, Inc.
29 East 21st Street, New York, NY 10010

Library of Congress Cataloging-in-Publication Data

Freedman, Jeri.
Women in the workplace: wages, respect, and equal rights / Jeri Freedman. — 1st ed.
   p. cm. — (A young woman's guide to contemporary issues)
Includes bibliographical references and index.
ISBN 978-1-4358-3541-2 (library binding)
1. Women employees. 2. Sex discrimination in employment. I. Title.
HD6053.F734 2009
331.4—dc22

2009013720

Manufactured in Malaysia
CPSIA Compliance Information: Batch #TW10YA: For Further Information contact Rosen Publishing, New York,
New York at 1-800-237-9932

Contents

INTRODUCTION

Since World War II (1939–1945), women have entered the workforce in ever-increasing numbers. According to the U.S. Department of Labor, women now account for 46 percent of the workforce, and nearly half of all new jobs created in the economy today go to women. One might expect that being represented in such numbers would guarantee women equality at work. However, despite their numbers, women still face inequality in terms of pay and

opportunity in the workplace.

Even now, many male managers have reservations about hiring and promoting women, especially for high-level positions. Women are still routinely offered lower starting salaries and are paid less than men doing the same work in the same position. There are a number of reasons for such differences, which are explored in this book.

In addition to unequal treatment on the job, women are vulnerable to sexual harassment—ranging from unwelcome advances to off-color jokes and snide remarks from men who resent or are threatened by their presence.

Many of the reasons for the unequal treatment of women stem from society's attitudes toward women, many of them with roots far back in history. Therefore, this book begins with a look at the history of women and work, and the attitudes that society held about them. It then explains the types of unequal treatment that women receive, including issues of unequal opportunity, unequal pay, and sexual harassment.

Despite the continuing obstacles, some progress has been made by working women over the past few decades, and a number of laws have been passed to help women in the workplace. These are explained, and some practical advice is provided on how to deal with issues of unequal treatment and sexual harassment in the workplace. The book concludes with a look at some of the trends that are likely to affect women in the workplace in the future.

CHAPTER 1

Women in the Workplace

Attitudes toward women and work today are shaped by centuries of cultural and religious attitudes. The ways that women and their work were viewed in earlier times have had a lasting influence on how many people view women in the workplace today. To provide a sense of how modern attitudes toward women in the workplace developed, this chapter and the next one examine these issues throughout history.

Women's Work in Preindustrial Times

In the early days of America and Canada, men and women generally worked together in family businesses. On the frontier, farming was the predominant enterprise, both in the colonies and later, in the early 1800s, during the expansion into the western part of North America. This meant that strength and hardiness were the most desirable traits for both women and men. Women cared for the

home and for children, and men were more likely to be involved in jobs requiring physical strength, such as building barns. But people of both genders cleared land, planted crops, and tended livestock.

THIS PHOTO, TAKEN AROUND 1900, SHOWS WOMEN WORKING IN A FACTORY MAKING SILK HATS. MAKING CLOTHES WAS SEEN AS AN EXTENSION OF WOMEN'S NATURAL WORK. THE CONDITIONS IN SUCH SWEATSHOPS WERE CRAMPED AND HARSH.

Off the farm, men were likely to be active in trades that earned significant money, such as shipbuilding, brewing, printing, and merchant shipping. Women were primarily involved in caring for the home and for children. There were a limited number of trades that were primarily engaged in by women. Women were milliners, who made hats, and seamstresses, who made clothing items for sale, such as aprons and shirts. Women also made items for sale, such as candles and soap. Businesses like these were seen as acceptable for women because they were a natural outgrowth of "women's work." However, men ran the major businesses. Because men made most of the money, they retained most of the power and ran the business of the colonies and the countries that grew out of them.

THE INDUSTRIAL AGE

Prior to the mid-nineteenth century, most work that women performed was done inside the home, performed in someone else's home, or was an extension of traditional women's work done outside the home. In-home work consisted of doing laundry or sewing, providing child care, or taking in boarders. Through the first quarter of the twentieth century, it was common for both middle-class and upper-class households to employ servants. Many women served as maids, cooks, and other household help, either on a live-in or daily basis, often beginning employment as young girls. Even nurses in hospitals were basically servants whose job it was to clean up and tend to patients' basic needs.

The Industrial Revolution changed the way that many women—and men—worked. The Industrial Revolution started near the end of the eighteenth century. The term refers to the rise of technology that led to the shift from making things by hand to making them by machines in

THIS PHOTO SHOWS A THREAD SPINNER WORKING AT A TEXTILE MILL IN FALL RIVER, MASSACHUSETTS, AROUND 1916. GIRLS OFTEN STARTED WORKING IN MILLS AT A YOUNG AGE.

factories. The Industrial Revolution changed the way people lived and worked. Prior to the Industrial Revolution, most goods were made by individual craftspeople and sold or bartered for goods locally. Now, for the first time, people who owned factories and employed large numbers of people as workers controlled the production of goods. The chance to work in the city attracted workers from farms and small towns. Factories also provided a means of livelihood to the flood of immigrants who came to the United States and Canada during the nineteenth and early twentieth centuries. Women were not limited to "women's work." Even in the nineteenth century, women were documented as working in five hundred different trades, including driving carts and being bridge keepers. However, most women who were employed outside the home generally worked in traditional female areas, such as laundries or textile factories. In the mid-1800s, the predominant occupation for women was servant, followed by the sewing and textile trades. Many worked in textile mills, where cloth was made, and in clothing factories. Prior to World War II, women were generally prohibited from learning many skills necessary for obtaining better-paying jobs that were occupied by men—and from applying for such jobs. This allowed factory owners to guarantee a pool of workers who had no choice but to work for low pay, which benefited the owners by reducing costs and increasing profits.

A second group of women who worked outside the home were those in the retail trade (selling goods to people). In the preindustrial period, when most shops

FACTORIES, SWEATSHOPS, AND PIECEWORK

In the nineteenth and early twentieth centuries, work in factories was harsh. Women, often young girls, frequently worked extremely long hours. The factories were often poorly heated in the winter and sweltering in the summer. In the days before labor and workplace safety laws, factories were often dangerous places to work. Such factories, where employees were forced to work long hours in terrible conditions over which they had no control, were called sweatshops. There were no protections or insurance for workers, and if one became injured, she was simply dismissed to fend for herself.

The largest area of employment for women in the nineteenth and early twentieth centuries, aside from being a servant, was working in the sewing trades. In textile mills, where cloth was made, 60 percent of the workers were girls and women. And in many clothing factories, all or most of the workers were female—although supervisors were male. As far as the factory owners were concerned, women were the ideal employees for tasks that required dexterity (skill with one's hands) and attention to detail, rather than brute strength. In addition, women were willing to work for lower wages than men, which was appealing to mill and factory owners. And women were raised to be docile, so they were unlikely to make trouble over their working conditions.

were family-owned, women worked alongside their husbands in businesses like inns and shops selling pottery, clothing, food, and other such goods. As the industrial age brought increasing prosperity to a growing middle class, the demand for goods increased. Many family businesses, such as Macy's, grew into major commercial enterprises, and new stores were opened to meet the rising demand. Women were rarely seen in managerial positions in these businesses. Instead, they were hired as "shopgirls," whose job it was to stand behind counters in department stores, be charming, and sell items to customers. Again, as their job was waiting on customers, they were still placed in servant-like roles.

PERCEPTIONS OF WOMEN IN THE WORKPLACE

The view that a man's role was to work outside the home and earn money, and a woman's role was to take care of the home and children and provide support for her man, influenced how women were perceived in the workplace. The predominant attitude in the industrial age was that women's work was temporary. They would leave to get married or raise children, which was viewed by most people as women's proper work. For example, both young men and young women might be hired to work as salespeople in department stores, but when a chance for promotion came up, the young man would be chosen because the boss assumed that the girl would eventually leave to get married. Indeed, it was considered socially unacceptable for a wealthy or middle-class woman to work because this implied that her husband was unable to support her, which made him look bad. If a woman wished to do something outside the home, she was expected to engage in charity work.

A WOMAN SELLS BALLOONS FOR CHARITY AT A 1922 SOCIETY FAIR IN NEW YORK CITY. SUCH ACTIVITIES WERE CONSIDERED ACCEPTABLE FOR WOMEN BECAUSE THEY DID NOT THREATEN MEN'S JOBS.

As with many stereotypes, the view of why women worked was at odds with reality. Whereas middle-class and upper-class women had the option of devoting their time to home and family, millions of working-class women had no choice but to raise children and work, either in factories or by taking in work at home. Maintaining the myth that women did not need to work helped protect better-paying jobs for men. Keeping women dependent on men also guaranteed that men would have someone at home to take care of their needs, leaving them free to pursue their activities outside the home.

CHAPTER 2

WOMEN'S WORK IN MODERN TIMES

T he modern role of women in the workforce has its roots in World War II. During World War II, women entered the mainstream workforce in large numbers for the first time. Because so many men were in the military, there was a shortage of workers in many jobs. In addition, when the United States entered the war, it needed vast amounts of supplies and equipment. At the same time that factories were gearing up to increase production, they were losing a large percentage of their mainly male workforce. Women were encouraged to step up to fill those jobs. "Rosie the Riveter" became the new symbol of the American woman pitching in to keep the wartime economy going, doing her patriotic duty to support the war effort by working in jobs that ranged from office work to assembling parts for aircraft and other military equipment. Rosie was actually Rose Will Monroe, a riveter at the Willow Run Aircraft factory in Ypsilanti, Michigan. She was featured in a promotional film and poster campaign. The number of

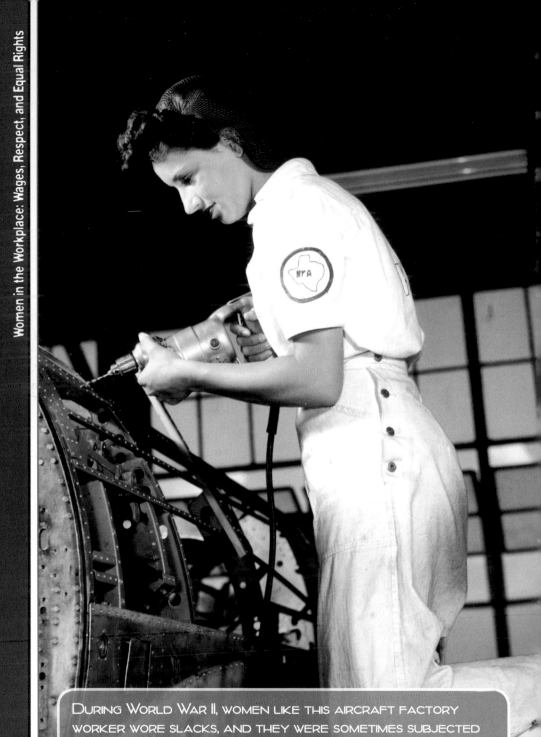

During World War II, women like this aircraft factory worker wore slacks, and they were sometimes subjected to sexist remarks by men on the street, who thought they weren't "ladies."

women in the workforce increased 57 percent from 1940 to 1944.

Many of the women who took jobs were young, and working helped shape their attitudes about themselves. Entering the workforce had two effects on American women: it gave them a sense of self-confidence that they could indeed do many jobs as well as men, despite having been told for generations that they couldn't, and it gave them financial independence—they could buy their own necessities and treat themselves to things that they wanted. Despite attempts in the 1950s to turn back the clock, as discussed in the next section, attitudes were being changed forever. Equal work didn't mean equal pay, however. In 1942, the National War Board pressured companies to voluntarily increase the pay for women to the rate paid to men when they were doing the same jobs with the same quality. Most companies were more interested in their profits than in women's rights, so they refused to voluntarily increase the pay rate for female workers. Women's pay remained unequal.

THE POSTWAR YEARS: 1950s

The influx of women into the workplace didn't last, however. The end of the war brought waves of men returning from the military to civilian life—and they wanted jobs. In many cases, women were dismissed from their jobs to make way for the returning men. Because there were no legal protections, many companies gave preference to men over women applying for the same jobs. The government asked women to voluntarily give

Many 1950s TV shows, such as *Father Knows Best*, presented the father as the "king" of the family with everyone catering to his needs, while the mother's job was to care for everyone.

up their jobs to returning soldiers. As wartime production shut down, the number of jobs shrank. The government feared that if women kept jobs, there wouldn't be enough for men, and this high unemployment would lead to a depression (a period in which business declines because people can't afford to buy goods). In addition, many women left the workforce to have children now that the war was over and their husbands had returned, creating the baby boom generation. Television shows such as *Father Knows Best*, *Leave It to Beaver*, and others promoted the image of the perfect family with a stay-at-home mother taking care of her husband and children.

Nonetheless, women's attitudes toward working were changing, and a quarter of married women continued to work outside the home. By 1956, 35 percent of the workforce was women. However, working did not mean equality. Those girls and women who did work in the 1950s were paid on average 59 to 64 cents for every dollar a man earned. Companies claimed that men had to support families, while women only needed money for luxuries.

AFFIRMATIVE ACTION

The 1950s were a prosperous time for many Americans — especially if they were white, male, and middle class. Members of minority groups, especially African Americans, didn't share in this prosperity. Segregation (keeping black people separate from white people) was legal. African Americans were not allowed into many facilities that were used by whites, and those that were provided for them were often inferior. In addition, they were denied many opportunities that were available only to white people. In response to this injustice, the civil rights movement formed with the goal of gaining equal treatment under the law for African Americans. After many violent confrontations and legal actions, a number of laws were enacted, eliminating segregation and outlawing discrimination on the basis of gender as well as color. Passing a law and changing social attitudes so that people comply with the spirit of the law are two different matters, however. Although antidiscrimination laws enacted in the 1960s forbade discrimination in hiring, many managers and companies continued to hire primarily white men for managerial and professional positions. Women and minorities had a hard time getting hired for, or being promoted to, high-paying positions. But proving discrimination was very difficult. Choosing a

THESE UNIVERSITY STUDENTS ARE DEMONSTRATING IN SUPPORT OF AFFIRMATIVE ACTION. ALTHOUGH ITS FUTURE IS HOTLY DEBATED, AFFIRMATIVE ACTION HAS HELPED ADVANCE WOMEN AND MINORITIES IN THE WORKPLACE.

candidate to hire or promote is often a matter of personal judgment, which makes it difficult to prove in court that a candidate was not chosen because of gender or color. Nonetheless, it was easy to document that women, blacks, and members of other minority groups were under-represented at higher levels of responsibility. Therefore, the federal government instituted affirmative action.

Affirmative action refers to the set of formal programs legislated by the federal government that are designed to increase the number of women and minorities hired to the same level as whites and men. A similar initiative enacted in Canada is called employment equity. Affirmative action regulations do not require companies to hire women at all costs. They merely require that when two candidates are equally qualified, the woman or minority candidate be given preference until a reasonable percentage of employees are women or minorities. Those in favor of affirmative action believe it is crucial to ensuring that women and minorities are given equal opportunity because many people are still prejudiced against them. Opponents of affirmative action claim that it is sometimes unfair to white male candidates, and that, although while it served a purpose at one time, times have changed and it is no longer necessary.

THE WOMEN'S MOVEMENT, CIVIL RIGHTS, AND EQUAL PAY

According to the Affirmative Action Review of 1995 by senior adviser to the president for policy and strategy

WOMEN IN THE WORKFORCE-STATISTICS

There are approximately 229 million people over the age of sixteen in the civilian population of the United States, of which about 118 million are women and 111 million are men.

There are about 153 million people in the workforce or looking for work, including 71 million women and 82 million men. The following are some statistics from the U.S. Department of Labor about women in the workforce from 1997 to 2007:

- Women make up about 46 percent of the workforce.
- 59.3 percent of women work, compared to 73.2 percent of men.
- 59 percent of Caucasian women, 61.1 percent of African American women, 58.6 percent of Hispanic women, and 58.6 of Asian women in the United States work.
- 63 percent of women with children under age six work.
- 60 percent of women with children under age three work.
- 48 percent of the 16 million new jobs that were created between 1997 and 2007 went to women.
- 3.8 million women hold more than one job.
- 75 percent of employed women work full-time; 25 percent work part-time.
- 66 percent of part-time workers are women.
- 45 percent of government employees are women.
- 3.6 million women are self-employed.

George Stephanopoulos and special counsel to the president Christopher Edley Jr., from the early 1900s to the mid-1970s, women earned on average about 60 percent of what men earned. Much of this difference

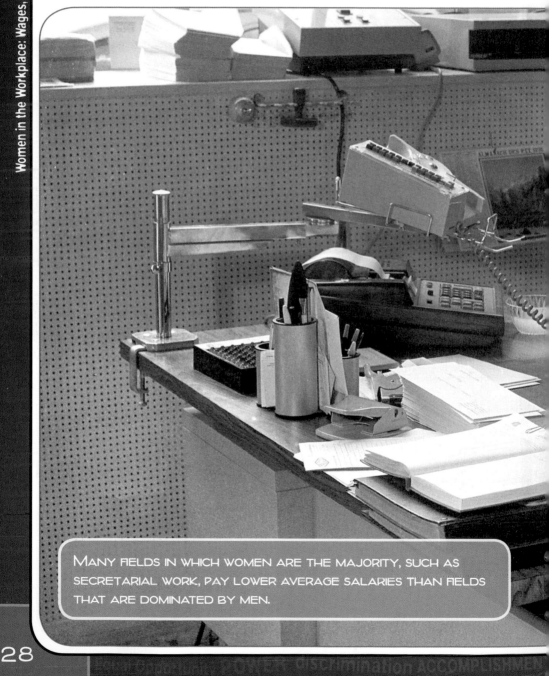

MANY FIELDS IN WHICH WOMEN ARE THE MAJORITY, SUCH AS SECRETARIAL WORK, PAY LOWER AVERAGE SALARIES THAN FIELDS THAT ARE DOMINATED BY MEN.

in earnings is attributable to the fact that women were in lower-paying jobs.

Throughout most of the twentieth century, girls and women were restricted to low-paying jobs. Prior to the

1970s, women in some states were forbidden by law from employment in certain fields, such as firefighting, police work, and mining. In some cities, women were prohibited from even applying for jobs as police officers or firefighters, and this was completely legal. Want ads often specified that applicants had to be male.

There were no laws to protect girls and women from sexual harassment or from being fired simply because they got married or became pregnant. On one hand, male managers often assumed that women would leave if they got married or pregnant in order to take care of their children. On the other hand, women were often fired for a variety of reasons if they became pregnant or got married. For instance, many men felt that women should have children and devote themselves to taking care of them if they were married. They also believed that women wouldn't dedicate themselves to their jobs as fully if they also had a family. In certain professions, such as teaching, it was considered inappropriate to have pregnant women in front of children because it raised issues relating to sex. Finally, many

men considered it OK for a woman to work if she was single because she had to support herself. But if she got married, she'd have a husband to support her, and continuing to work meant that she was taking a job from a man who might have a family to support.

Although laws prohibiting employment discrimination were passed in the 1960s, it wasn't until the late 1970s that women really started to make progress in the

THESE WOMEN ARE MARCHING FOR EQUAL RIGHTS AT A 1971 DEMONSTRATION. BEGINNING IN THE 1960s, WOMEN STARTED DEMANDING THE RIGHT TO EMPLOYMENT OPPORTUNITIES AND PAY EQUAL TO THOSE OF MEN.

workplace, achieving better jobs and higher pay. One reason for this was that changing the law is often not sufficient to achieve a major cultural change in attitudes. For example, if a girl applied for an after-school job at a hardware store or garage, she would be hired only for a position as a cashier because it was assumed that she didn't know anything about using tools. It is also necessary to change the way that society views a group of people such as women and—often more important—the way that people view themselves. This is the role played by the women's movement.

The women's movement, or the feminist movement, refers to the organized efforts of women from the nine-teenth century to the present to change social attitudes about women and obtain equal treatment for them in areas such as work. The fight to secure the right to vote is known as the "first wave" of feminism, and the women's movement in the 1960s and 1970s is known as the "second wave." The debate over fairness in the workplace is not new. As far back as 1923, women's rights advocates hotly debated women's wages. That year, in *Adkins v. Children's Hospital*, the U.S. Supreme Court struck down a Washington, D.C., law that set a minimum wage for women workers. The Court ruled that the law was unconstitutional because if one allowed the state to set a minimum wage, it could also theoretically set a maximum wage, and setting a specific wage interfered with the right of people to freely negotiate their pay. Women's rights advocates were arrayed on both sides of the argument, some arguing that the D.C. law at least guaranteed the women workers a minimum wage and others fearing it would lead to a set, lower rate of pay for women.

In more recent times, the women's movement has played a key role in obtaining the passage of laws protecting women against sexual harassment and abuse, and granting them equal opportunity and pay in the workplace. Some feminist texts, like Betty Friedan's *The Feminine Mystique* (1963), contributed to the shift in culture in the postwar era that resulted in more women seeking paid work and the second wave of the feminist movement.

CHAPTER 3

EQUAL OPPORTUNITY

Equal opportunity means having an equal chance to be hired for a job and promoted. It means equal treatment in the workplace for women and men. Unfortunately, equal treatment is something women have yet to achieve.

HIRING ISSUES

The first hurdle that girls and women face in the workplace is getting hired. The key law that protects women's rights in the workplace is Title VII of the Civil Rights Act of 1964 (usually just referred to as Title VII). This act covers employees of businesses with fifteen or more employees and state and local government agencies. It doesn't cover federal government employees or outside contractors. Title VII prohibits discrimination based on race, skin color, gender, religious beliefs, or national origin. Such discrimination applies to hiring, promotions, work assignments, benefits, and virtually every other aspect of employment.

Unfortunately, girls and women often have to send out more résumés, respond to more ads, and attend more interviews to obtain a job. In many cases, women are also offered less for a given job than a male candidate, possibly because of the belief on the part of the manager doing the hiring that women will accept less money than a male candidate. Some of the reasons for this are discussed in the next chapter.

In regard to hiring, it is illegal for potential employers to ask certain questions that could lead to discriminating against a woman because of characteristics related to the fact that she is a woman. Among these questions are those related to the following:

- Age, which could be used to see if a woman is of childbearing age, among other things; employers may ask if a person is a minimum age for jobs that require it, such as serving alcohol.
- Pregnancy, such as, "Do you plan to have children?"
- Family, such as, "Do you have children?" and "Do you have people at home you take care of?" They can ask if a person is available for certain shifts or time frames.
- Marital status, such as, "Are you married?" and "Do you plan to get married?"
- Height or weight; they can ask if a person is able to carry out specific required physical tasks.

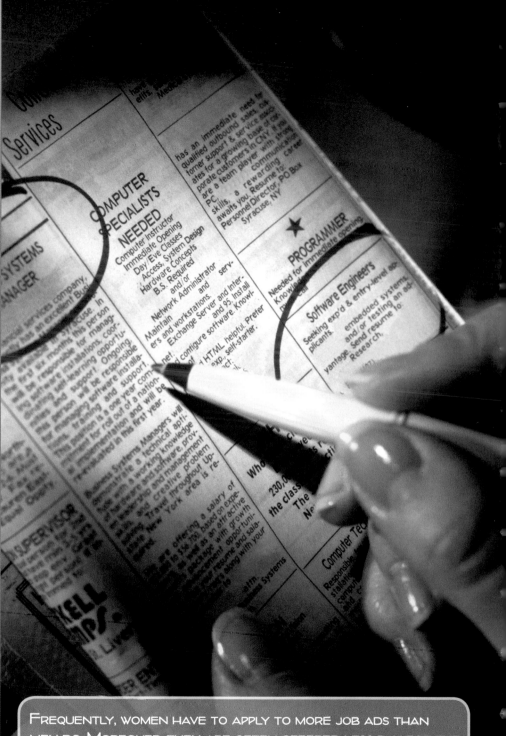

FREQUENTLY, WOMEN HAVE TO APPLY TO MORE JOB ADS THAN MEN DO. MOREOVER, THEY ARE OFTEN OFFERED LESS PAY FOR THE SAME JOB THAN MALE CANDIDATES.

What is the best way for a person to respond if she is asked an illegal question? Responding in a defensive way is likely to keep her from getting the job. The best way is to answer the question behind the question. In other words, if someone asks a person if she has children at home that she has to take care of, the best answer is probably something like, "I understand that the job may require me to work hours other than strictly nine to five, and I'm prepared for that." If the question, although illegal, was asked out of legitimate concern that the individual might be running out the door the minute the clock strikes five, when that person may still be needed, that answer should address the issue. If the interviewer keeps asking inappropriate questions, however, that may indicate a prejudicial attitude toward hiring a woman.

THE PROMOTION PROBLEM

Once a woman has a job, she has to deal with the issue of advancement. All too often, unfortunately, girls and women run into discrimination when it comes to promotions. In August 2004, Jon Bonné wrote an article for MSNBC.com that provides an overview of a number of recent studies shedding light on the differences between the opportunities for men and women in corporations.

One issue that affects the promotion of women in corporations is their attitude. In general, women are more likely than men to be brought up to think about others, whereas boys are raised to think about

ONE OF THE CHALLENGES WOMEN FACE IS BALANCING THE DEMANDS OF FAMILY AND THEIR JOB DURING THE YEARS WHEN THEY ARE MOST LIKELY TO BE COMPETING FOR ADVANCEMENT AT WORK.

achievement. Boys are constantly pushed into competing and winning. This plays out in the corporate world as well. The research firm ISR conducted a four-year study. As part of the survey, 2,888 senior executives and 31,945 middle managers were interviewed. ISR found that men were more focused than women on their own advancement and moving up the ladder, whereas women were more likely to be concerned about their coworkers and customers.

Interestingly, women in middle management were more likely than men to worry about balancing home life and work. But at the senior management level, men were more likely than women to be worried by this. Bonné suggests that age may be a key element in this fact. Women are typically in middle management when they are in their thirties and, therefore, likely to have young children. Like it or not, women still bear the brunt of child rearing responsibilities, even when they work. By the time most people reach senior management, they are middle-aged. Many middle-aged women are free of responsibilities for raising children. At the same time, many middle-aged men, who have devoted their entire lives to their job, start to feel a need for other types of fulfillment, including spending more time with their family. However, it is also true that a larger proportion of women than men who make it to senior management are unmarried or divorced.

The fact that women accounted for 45 percent of middle managers in the companies surveyed but only 25 percent of senior executives supports the idea that those doing the promoting favor male managers over female ones.

Another study released in 2004 by Catalyst (an organization that seeks to advance women's role in business) revealed that at Fortune 1000 companies, male and female senior managers were equally likely to compete for CEO jobs. Yet women still represented only a quarter of senior managers. In a related survey of managers at global companies, ISR found that women less frequently felt they were given adequate details about their company's strategic goals. And while 82 percent of men felt management made fair decisions, only 68 percent of women shared that view.

THE GLASS CEILING

The "glass ceiling" refers to an invisible barrier that stops a woman's upward progress. In business, this refers to a barrier that keeps a woman from being promoted beyond a certain level simply because she is female. The barrier is invisible because it is not an official policy but discrimination resulting from the personal prejudices and opinions of senior management. Often, this barrier becomes apparent when a woman has advanced to a certain level, usually middle management.

In a 2006 study published in the *Journal of Applied Psychology*, Karen S. Lyness and Madeline E. Heilman examined 448 women managers. They found that women were promoted to senior management less frequently than men. Beyond that, they found that women who were promoted to senior management had better performance reviews than men who were promoted, and their promotion was more closely tied to outstanding performance. What this implies is that a man may be promoted to the highest levels for many reasons. He may be perceived as having "what it takes" or "leadership qualities." For a woman to get promoted, her performance must be extraordinary

The authors of the study suggested that one reason for the difficulty women have with breaking into senior management is the perception on the part of those running the company, or sitting on the board of directors, that women have certain stereotypical characteristics that would

WOMEN OFTEN REACH MIDDLE MANAGEMENT LEVEL, BUT ONLY A SMALL PERCENTAGE OF WOMEN ARE PROMOTED TO SENIOR MANAGEMENT. EVEN FEWER REACH THE CEO LEVEL OF COMPANIES THEY DON'T OWN.

interfere with their ability to perform at the highest levels of management. Examples of such stereotypes are "women are emotional" and "women will put their families before their job." Women are seen as "caring" and "relationship-oriented," but men are seen as tough and aggressive—attitudes that men doing the promoting see as critical to succeeding. The authors showed that stereotypical assumptions about women colored the way that senior management evaluated women. They tended to interpret women's behavior in the workplace in light of what they assumed about women. In other words, if a man goes out of his way to show a subordinate how to do something, he's being a mentor; if a woman does so, she's being caring or "touchy-feely." Thus, similar behavior is interpreted differently according to gender. Or if a man objects strongly to something, he's seen as being "forceful" or "assertive," whereas a woman doing the same thing is seen as being "unreasonable" or "overemotional." Thus, biased attitudes work against women in two ways. A woman faces the assumption that she doesn't have "what it takes" based on preconceptions by senior management. This view is then justified by her performance reviews, in which her behavior is interpreted according to these same preconceptions.

Breaking through the glass ceiling is very difficult, and women in this position are often faced with hard choices. Should they try to behave like the stereotype of a man—in a very aggressive and tough fashion? Should they admit that they have no chance of getting promoted and go to another company or start their own business? Should they attempt to collect evidence of discrimination and try to implement a complaint through the Equal

> ONE OF THE FRUSTRATING ELEMENTS OF "PINK-COLLAR GHETTO" JOBS IS THAT THEY HAVE NO CAREER PATH. WOMEN MAY BE STUCK IN MINIMUM OR LOW-WAGE JOBS FOR YEARS.

Employment Opportunity Commission (EEOC) or a lawsuit for discrimination? Unfortunately, the only real remedy for the glass ceiling is a change in attitudes throughout society so that people are valued equally for their skills, regardless of gender.

THE PINK-COLLAR GHETTO

The "pink-collar ghetto" refers to the pool of low-paying, dead-end jobs in fields populated mostly by girls and women. This category includes jobs such as waitress, grocery store cashier, child care worker, nurse's aide, clerical worker, house and office cleaner, and hotel housekeeping staff, among others.

One aspect that pink-collar jobs have in common is that they are seen as "women's work." Another is that the pay is frequently low and benefits often limited or nonexistent. One reason why pay is low is that this type of work frequently involves serving or caring for people, and such work is looked down upon in our society. Another is that women are often desperate to find work to pay their bills but possess few job skills. Therefore, they will take jobs at low pay that men will not. A third reason is that even unskilled men can often find higher-paying work in jobs that are dangerous or require physical strength, like construction or mining. Such industries may have difficulty finding people willing to do dangerous, physically demanding work and so must pay higher wages. Even when men and women do essentially the same job, women's jobs are frequently presented as less significant, reflecting their different status in American society. Thus, a man who cleans a building is a janitor, but a woman who does so is a cleaning lady or maid—and it's likely that the man is paid more.

Because the pay for women is so low in the pink-collar ghetto, many women must work two or even three jobs to make ends meet. Having to work so much, and often care for children as well, means they do not have the time to learn new skills that would lead to better jobs, even if they had the money to attend classes.

Because skilled and semiskilled jobs in trades that are primarily male pay as much as 30 percent more than jobs in predominately female fields, the U.S. government passed the Nontraditional Employment for Women (NEW) Act of 1991. This act requires state job-training agencies to put in place programs to train women for nontraditional jobs, for example, carpentry or truck driving. Nontraditional fields are defined as those where less than 25 percent of those employed are women.

THE MOMMY TRACK

The "mommy track" refers to an alternate career path for women in their prime who must raise children as well as work. Many women must make a choice that men do not. Do they devote themselves fully to their career, or do they devote themselves primarily to the children and merely work to earn money? Many women choose to take time off to have children and care for them while they are growing up. Those who need to work as well as care for a family must still take time off from their jobs or work fewer hours, which reduces their chances of advancement in corporate life.

Many companies have taken steps to keep talented female employees who have family responsibilities. These

CORPORATE DAY-CARE FACILITIES, SUCH AS THE ONE PICTURED HERE, ALLOW WOMEN TO SPEND TIME WITH THEIR CHILDREN DURING THE WORKDAY AND ELIMINATE THE NFED TO PICK UP THE CHILDREN SOMEWHERE ELSE.

include elements such as providing for child care, offering flexible hours, and allowing employees to work remotely over a computer from home. While these steps are beneficial in that they help women retain professional positions in the workplace, nonetheless, the mommy track is a road that forks away from the executive suite. Women on the mommy track are unlikely to be promoted to high levels of authority because these jobs are considered to require a greater level of availability to the business and a willingness to work whatever hours are necessary to achieve a goal.

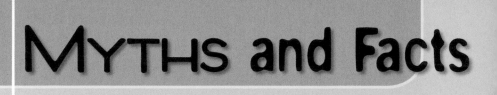

MYTHS and Facts

MYTH

Since the number of women in middle management has been steadily increasing, women and men will eventually reach equality in the workplace.

Fact

A 2007 survey by the consulting firm Grant Thornton reveals that only 38 percent of businesses worldwide have women in senior management (vice president, chief executive officer, and chief operating officer positions). And the number in the United States has dropped 6 percent since 2004. In 2009, only thirteen Fortune 500 companies had female CEOs.

MYTH

If you work hard and do a good job, you will be promoted.

Fact

Doing good work is not enough. Management's attitudes and corporate "politics" often play a major role in who gets promoted to key positions. Women need to learn how to present themselves and their accomplishments in order to gain the attention of key management.

MYTH

Nowadays, working men and women share
household and child care tasks equally.

Fact

A 2004 U.S. Department of Labor survey found that
working women spend seven more hours per week
on housework than men, and they spend twice
as much time per day on child care.

CHAPTER 4

EQUAL PAY FOR EQUAL WORK

The "wage gap" is a statistical measure of the difference between the average pay for women and men. According to the Current Population Survey report by the U.S. Department of Labor Statistics, the median earnings in 2007 for women employed full-time in hourly and salaried jobs were approximately $31,900, or 80 percent of the median earnings for men, which were approximately $39,800. Interestingly, among workers paid by the hour, women earned 85 percent of what men earned. This amount indicates that difference in pay is greater among white-collar jobs, where pay rates are dependent to a greater extent on the choice of field, the candidate's ability to negotiate his or her pay, and the manager's subjective impression of the employees and their work. The previous chapter discussed the way in which prejudice on the part of male managers often blocks women's progress. There are, however, a number of other factors that affect a woman's obtaining equal pay.

Demonstrators show their support for the Paycheck Fairness Act and Lilly Ledbetter Fair Pay Act. The latter act was passed in 2009, but the struggle for equal pay continues.

CHOICE OF FIELDS

Some aspects of employment that affect pay are within a woman's control. One of the reasons for the disparity between how much men and women make is the type of fields in which women work. The following is a 2007 list from the U.S. Department of Labor of the top ten professions in which women are employed. Many of the jobs chosen by women, such as teaching, place a high premium on emotional fulfillment and a sense of contribution at the expense of less-fulfilling, higher-paying jobs that might be found in business and industry. The top ten professions include the following:

1. Secretaries and administrative assistants (3,289,000)
2. Registered nurses (2,411,000)
3. Elementary and middle school teachers (2,381,000)
4. Cashiers (2,285,000)
5. Retail salespersons (1,798,000)
6. Nursing, psychiatric, and home health aides (1,659,000)
7. First-line supervisors/managers of retail sales workers (1,468,000)
8. Waitresses (1,464,000)
9. Bookkeeping, accounting, and auditing clerks (1,345,000)
10. Receptionists and information clerks (1,340,000)

THE WAGE GAP-STATISTICS

The following are some key statistics regarding the wage gap. In 2007, only 7.5 percent of women made $1,500/week ($78,000/year), compared to 16 percent of men. At the same time, 3.8 percent of women earned $150/week or less ($7,800/year), compared to 2.2 percent of men. And 14.6 percent of women earned $250/week or less ($13,000/year), compared to 8.7 percent of men.

The wage gap increases with age. According to the 2007 Comparative Pay Survey by the U.S. Census Bureau, women ages sixteen to twenty-four earned 92 percent as much as men, women ages twenty-four to thirty-four earned 87.7 percent as much, women ages thirty-five to forty-four earned 77 percent, and women over forty-five earned 73 percent as much. There has actually been an improvement in the wage gap over time. In 1979, when the Labor Department started tracking this information, the median pay for all women was only 62 percent of the median pay for men, and women ages thirty-five to fifty-four earned only 57 to 58 percent of what men earned. However, there is still an obvious difference in the amounts that men and women are paid. In Canada, the Department of Human Resources Development oversees wage and discrimination issues. A 2000 report by the Canadian government on gender composition and wages claimed that women's wages were closer to men's in Canada than in the United States, which was true at the time. However, according to the report, women's wages were still lower than men's wages, with women earning 75 to 80 percent of what men earned. This ratio is about the same as the difference between women's and men's wages in the United States today.

In 2004, women were 46 percent of the U.S. workforce and 48.6 percent of those in the workforce with college degrees, according to the National Science Foundation. However, they represented only 24.7 percent of people working in science and engineering. Because science and engineering jobs typically have high pay ranges, the lack of women in such fields has a significant impact on the average pay of women overall.

THE COMFORT FACTOR

When it comes to getting hired, obtaining equal pay, or being promoted, women faced with a male manager are often at a disadvantage. People tend to feel most comfortable with people like themselves and give preference to such people. Even among men, a manager is most likely to reward those he sees as most like himself. In addition, many men still have preconceptions about women, as discussed earlier, and this affects the way they view their employees. Unfortunately, many men feel threatened by a strong or successful woman, and they react in a negative fashion.

GETTING PAID WHAT YOU'RE WORTH

The fact that the law says it is unfair to discriminate in matters of pay does not mean you can be assured that you are getting the same salary as your male coworkers. For jobs in which workers are paid an hourly wage, it is generally easy to establish what the pay rate is for people with similar years of experience and levels of performance.

JOBS IN SCIENCE ARE AMONG THE MOST HIGHLY PAID — AND AMONG THOSE IN THE MOST DEMAND. A WILLINGNESS TO STUDY SCIENCE CAN LEAD TO A BETTER-PAYING JOB.

When it comes to salaried workers, however, it is much more difficult to know how one's pay compares to colleagues'. Often, there is a large range for a given job, such as marketing manager, and in many businesses, how well you negotiate for a starting salary and for raises is the major factor influencing your pay.

IN A FIRST JOB, LIKE THIS SEVENTEEN-YEAR-OLD'S JOB AS A CASHIER, DOING AN OUTSTANDING JOB CAN HELP IN OBTAINING RECOMMENDATIONS THAT MAY CONTRIBUTE TO GETTING A FUTURE POSITION.

WHAT YOU CAN DO

One step you can take to protect yourself against discrimination on the job is document the job you're doing. Keep copies of any positive job reviews or evaluations, commendations, or letters from managers, clients, or

customers praising your work. Also, document any special achievements or contributions that you make to the company. For example, if you were the top salesperson for the year or came up with a procedure that saved the company a large sum of money, document this.

A company is under no obligation to spend more money than it has to. In fact, managers are often rewarded for keeping costs down. The fact is that one of the major reasons men make more money than women in the same position is that they ask for it. Women are often more

LEARNING TO PRESENT YOURSELF AND YOUR ACCOMPLISHMENTS IN A PROFESSIONAL AND POSITIVE MANNER IS A CRUCIAL SKILL FOR ADVANCING IN BUSINESS.

reluctant to confront managers about their pay because they don't like conflict, are afraid they may not be worth more, or have an unrealistic fear that they will lose their job if they ask for more. Let's address these issues.

First, if you ask for a raise, promotion, special assignment that's available, or anything else in a nonconfrontational and professional manner, it's unlikely that the discussion will turn unpleasant. You might get what you want or not, but if you can't have what you want, your manager will most likely explain why it's not possible. And you can accept that or take the next appropriate step.

It's also unlikely that you'll be fired for asking for more. It takes a lot of time and money to train someone for a position in an organization. If you're doing a good job, you're a useful asset to the company. For that reason, if your manager doesn't want to pay you more, he or she will most likely either explain why that's not possible or promise to review your situation at a later date. If the latter is the case, have your manger pencil in a precise date on the calendar so that you are not fobbed off with the same excuse every time you ask.

The issue of what one is worth is a more difficult one. It is a good idea to keep up with what typical pay ranges are for the job you do. You can find this information by checking help wanted ads, talking to colleagues in the same field, and checking salary surveys for your industry. Such surveys are often published annually by industry organizations and magazines that serve the industry. That said, what many women don't realize is that this question is entirely irrelevant. If you are doing a good job and haven't received a raise in some time, or if you find that other people in your position are making more, simply do what many men do: go to your boss, point this fact out (in a professional tone), show him or her your evidence of contribution, and ask for more.

Your documentation serves a second purpose, however. If you feel you have been unfairly passed over for a promotion or were given less of a raise than male coworkers in a similar position, you will have evidence to support your contention that your treatment is unjustified. The next chapter examines some of the protections and remedies available to women.

CHAPTER 5

Protections for Women in the Workplace

The Civil Rights Act of 1964 was landmark legislation that made it illegal to discriminate against women and minorities when hiring. In Canada, the Human Rights Act was passed in 1977 to ensure equal opportunity and outlaw discrimination on the basis of gender, disability, or religion, but it applies only to federally regulated industries. Each province is responsible for implementing its own antidiscrimination laws.

The Civil Rights Act of 1964 laid the groundwork for a number of major rulings by the U.S. Supreme Court that granted women legal protections in the workplace that they never had before, beginning in the 1970s.

In 1970, in *Schultz v. Wheaton Glass Co.*, the Court ruled that jobs do not have to be identical to qualify for equal pay; they merely have to be "substantially equivalent." This was a landmark case because it stopped employers from giving women different job titles and claiming that their jobs were different from jobs being done by men that were essentially the same.

PRESIDENT LYNDON B. JOHNSON SIGNS THE CIVIL RIGHTS ACT OF 1964 INTO LAW. AMONG OTHER ACTIONS, THIS LAW MADE IT ILLEGAL TO DISCRIMINATE AGAINST WOMEN IN THE WORKPLACE.

In 1971, in *Phillips v. Martin Marietta Corp.*, the Court ruled that a company could not refuse to hire women because they had preschool-aged children, unless it also refused to hire men who had them. This was a direct challenge to the concept that women shouldn't be hired because they would neglect their children to work, or neglect their work to take care of their children. That same year, in *Reed v. Reed*, the Court struck down an Illinois law that arbitrarily gave preference to men as to who should administer the estate of someone who died without a will. (The case involved the choice of a male parent over a female parent when it came to who should administer the estate of a deceased child.) The Court ruled that giving preference to a man over a woman in legal matters, when there was no legitimate reason for doing so, violated the Fourteenth Amendment, which guarantees equal protection under the law to all U.S. citizens.

In 1973, in *Pittsburgh Press Co. v. Pittsburgh Commission on Human Relations*, the Court upheld a municipal ordinance that forbade companies from specifying the gender of applicants in want ads for jobs. This was one of the most fundamental changes in hiring practices.

In 1974, in *Corning Glassworks v. Brennan*, the Court ruled that women could not be paid a lower wage than men simply because it was what they were customarily paid in the marketplace. This makes sense because this is exactly what the law was trying to address.

Both Congress and the Supreme Court were active in taking steps to reduce discrimination against women. The following are some of the major laws enacted to protect individuals' rights in the workplace—laws that directly affect women.

EEOC

As the civil rights struggle heightened in the 1960s, President John F. Kennedy announced plans to enact the Civil Rights Act. This was an omnibus bill (which means it contained many provisions) to address discrimination in voting, education, and employment, among other areas. Despite Kennedy's assassination in 1963, Congress passed the act and the Civil Rights Act of 1964 became law. Title VII of the act, which prohibited discrimination based on race, color, national origin, sex, and religion, created the Equal Employment Opportunity Commission (EEOC). The EEOC is charged with enforcing anti-discrimination laws relating to employment and resolving complaints of discrimination.

FEDERAL CONTRACT REGULATIONS

Also contributing to the hiring of an increasing number of women in business is Executive Order 11246, which is administered by the U.S. Labor Department's Office of Federal Contract Compliance Programs. This order requires firms that do business with the federal government to implement affirmative action and nondiscrimination measures if they want to obtain government contracts. Preference in awarding contracts is given to firms that take steps to hire more minorities and women. This legislation

If you feel that you have been discriminated against, you can file a claim with the Equal Employment Opportunity Commission (EEOC). Claims can be filed in person at an EEOC office or by phone. In areas where state or local agencies exist, you may be required to file a claim with them first. If this is the case, the filing deadline for the EEOC is extended while awaiting results from local agencies. A list of local EEOC offices is available on the Internet at http://www.eeoc.gov/offices.html.

has contributed to an increase in women in traditionally male industries, such as defense, energy, and construction, among others.

MATERNITY AND SICK LEAVE LAWS

The Pregnancy Discrimination Act, which is an amendment to the 1964 Civil Rights Act, prohibits discrimination against pregnant women. It makes it illegal to refuse to hire a woman because she is pregnant or to keep her from doing her normal job duties because she is pregnant. According to the EEOC, "In fiscal year 2007, EEOC received 5,587 charges of pregnancy-based discrimination. EEOC resolved 4,979 pregnancy discrimination charges in FY 2007 and recovered $30 million in monetary benefits for charging parties and other aggrieved individuals."

Another law that has been a help to women is the Family Leave and Medical Act. This law, passed in 1995, provides employees with up to twelve weeks of leave per

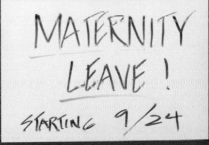

MATERNITY LEAVE !
STARTING 9/24

THE FAMILY LEAVE AND MEDICAL ACT GUARANTEES THAT WOMEN CAN TAKE MATERNITY LEAVE AND BE GUARANTEED THEIR JOB OR AN EQUIVALENT ONE WHEN THEY RETURN.

year for medical purposes, for themselves or to take care of a family member. During this time, the company is required to maintain their health care benefits. Upon completion of their leave, employees are entitled to have their job back

or receive an equivalent one. The law applies to state, local, and federal government agencies and companies with more than fifty employees. The provisions include maternity leave and leave to care for a newborn. Although

SURROUNDED BY MEMBERS OF CONGRESS AND LILLY LEDBETTER (THIRD FROM LEFT), PRESIDENT BARACK OBAMA SIGNS THE LILLY LEDBETTER FAIR PAY ACT ON JANUARY 29, 2009. THE ACT STRUCK DOWN THE 180-DAY LIMIT FOR FILING AN EQUAL PAY LAWSUIT.

it applies to male employees as well, it is particularly important for women because they are more likely to stay home with a newborn and be the one to care for a sick family member.

LILLY LEDBETTER FAIR PAY ACT

The Lilly Ledbetter Fair Pay Act was passed by Congress and was the first bill signed into law by President Barack Obama, on January 30, 2009. This bill removes the 180-day limitation on filing suits for discrimination when a woman is paid less than her male colleagues performing the same work. This means that if a woman found out that she had been receiving less pay for the same work for a period of years, she would be able to obtain compensation for past discrimination. A second bill that was passed by the U.S. House of Representatives in January 2009 is the Paycheck Fairness Act. This act would require an employer to pay women at the same rate as men for a given job unless the employer could demonstrate that there was a reason other than gender (education level, skills, or experience) that would justify a pay difference. Further, it would give women the right to sue for punitive damages, not just back pay. Punitive damages are those awarded to a plaintiff (the person who is suing) by a court as punishment of the defendant for breaking a law. At the time of this writing, the bill was still awaiting a vote in the U.S. Senate.

CHAPTER 6

Sexual Harassment

What is sexual harassment? According to the EEOC, sexual harassment is any unwelcome sexual advances or verbal or physical conduct that creates a hostile, threatening, or offensive work environment. It also includes any behavior that implies that not providing sexual favors will affect an employee's employment. Note that sexual harassment is more than just requests for sex. It also includes offensive comments and jokes and physical behavior. Failure of management to stop such behavior has been interpreted by courts as creating a hostile work environment for women who have to put up with it.

Here are a number of key points about sexual harassment:

- Sexual harassment is not dependent on gender. The harasser and victim can be of either gender.
- The harasser does not have to be a supervisor or even an employee of the company. A

manager, coworker, or non-employee like an outside contractor can engage in sexual harassment. It is up to the company to protect the employee from sexual harassment, regardless of the source.

- In addition to the person who is directly harassed, other people affected by the conduct may be considered victims of sexual harassment.
- Sexual harassment does not have to involve loss of money or job. Hostile or offensive behavior is

WOMEN HAVE A RIGHT NOT TO BE PHYSICALLY TOUCHED IN THE WORKPLACE. IF SOMEONE'S BEHAVIOR MAKES A WOMAN UNCOMFORTABLE, SHE HAS THE RIGHT TO ASK THAT PERSON TO STOP DOING IT.

still harassment, even if there is no financial cost
to the victim.

■ The behavior must be unwanted to be sexual
harassment. If two people are interested in each
other and decide to date, this is not illegal.
However, because such lines are not always clear,
one should be very careful about approaching
someone else in the workplace and consider
what might happen if the relationship doesn't
work out. It is rarely advisable for a supervisor to
approach a subordinate with a romantic interest.

If a person has been the victim of sexual harassment,
the first step is to contact someone in the company's human
resources department to discuss the incident.

How to Deal with Sexual Harassment

If you feel that someone is sexually harassing you or is behav-
ing inappropriately, there are certain steps you must take to
protect yourself both physically and legally. First, it is very
important to make it clear to the harasser that the behavior
is unwelcome. Many people have a juvenile or inappropriate
sense of humor, and their buddies often share this. If people
say things that are offensive to you, or they make off-color
jokes, tell them that you find those things offensive. If someone
approaches you inappropriately, make it clear that you are
not interested and/or object to that person's behavior. This
is important in establishing that the behavior is unwelcome.

Some people who engage in sexual harassment do a good job of hiding their behavior from management. Bringing it out in the open can help protect other women as well.

Once the incident is over, immediately write down what happened, when it happened, where it happened, who was present, and exactly what was said or done. That way, you will have all the facts and won't have to worry about forgetting the exact details of the incident.

Before you do anything else, discuss the situation with your employer. Companies have a vested interest in complying with the law. There are laws against sexual harassment, and the company has nothing to gain—and a lot to lose— by violating them. Do not assume that your boss or other members of management are aware that there is a problem. Start by informing them about the situation. Do so in a straightforward manner, without being confrontational. Take the approach that there is a problem and you want to work with management to resolve it.

Next, you should access whatever mechanism your company has to deal with sexual harassment. Your company should have a process for dealing with complaints about sexual harassment. The human resources department should be able to tell you exactly what you should do to file a complaint. (See the list of useful questions for discussing the situation with human resources on page 79.)

If the situation is not resolved appropriately, contact the EEOC for information on how to file a sexual harassment complaint, or consult a lawyer who deals with sexual harassment issues. Every company is required to have procedures in place to deal with sexual harassment and to take immediate steps to deal with it when it occurs. Failure to do so is cause for filing a sexual harassment suit. This should be your last step. If you need to file a suit, you will need to hire a lawyer.

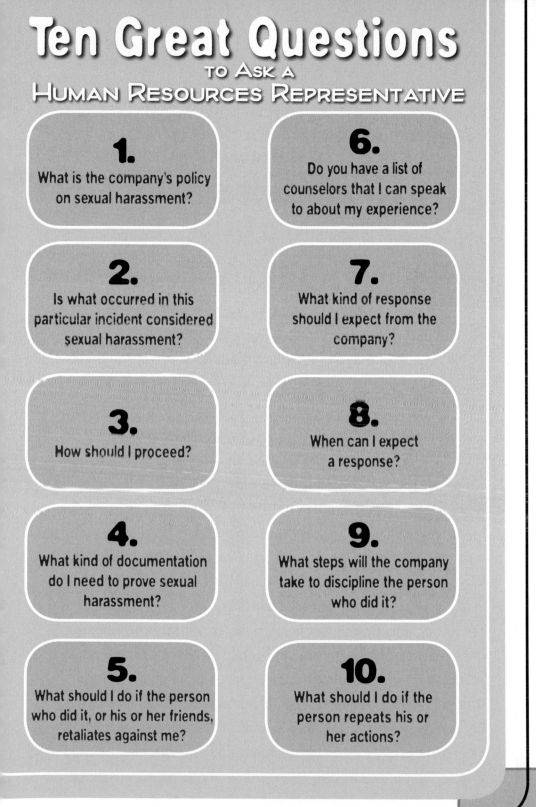

Ten Great Questions

TO ASK A
HUMAN RESOURCES REPRESENTATIVE

1.
What is the company's policy on sexual harassment?

2.
Is what occurred in this particular incident considered sexual harassment?

3.
How should I proceed?

4.
What kind of documentation do I need to prove sexual harassment?

5.
What should I do if the person who did it, or his or her friends, retaliates against me?

6.
Do you have a list of counselors that I can speak to about my experience?

7.
What kind of response should I expect from the company?

8.
When can I expect a response?

9.
What steps will the company take to discipline the person who did it?

10.
What should I do if the person repeats his or her actions?

CHAPTER 7

WOMEN IN THE MILITARY

W omen in the military face special issues in addition to those faced by civilian women. This chapter takes a look back at the rulings that affect the position of women in the military and explores specific issues facing women in the armed forces.

INTEGRATING WOMEN INTO THE MILITARY

On June 12, 1948, Congress passed the Women's Services Integration Act. This act allows women to serve as regular members of the U.S. Army, Navy, Marine Corps, and Air Force on the same footing as men. In 1951, Secretary of Defense George C. Marshall formed the Defense Department Advisory Committee on Women in the Services. This committee is still active, and it advises the Defense Department on regulations needed to ensure the proper recruiting, training, retaining, and employing of women, and ensuring the proper treatment of women in the military. The committee's recommendations have served as the basis for changes in many of the regulations and procedures in the military. The following are some of the committee's recommendations:

- In 1978, it recommended that the U.S. Navy and Marine Corps allow women to be commissioned as limited duty officers. A limited duty officer is someone who is promoted from the ranks because he or she possesses a certain technical skill that is needed. These officers are limited in the rank that they can advance to, hence the title limited duty officer. Prior to 1978, the Limited Duty Officer Program was open only to men.

- In 1979, it made two recommendations that affect women in the military today. These include the recommendation that the eligibility standards for women be the same as for men, except for obvious physical differences. In addition, there should be identical standards for promotion of men and women in the marines.

- In 1980, it recommended that the president of the United States give priority to the appointment of women as judges to the U.S. Court of Military Appeals. Currently, the court includes female judges, including one senior judge.

- In 1984, it recommended that the secretary of defense publish a formal policy requiring commanders to fully use women in their units.

- In 1992, it recommended that the secretary of defense allow women pilots in all military

LIEUTENANT COLONEL MARTHA MCSALLY WAS THE FIRST WOMAN IN THE U.S. AIR FORCE TO FLY IN COMBAT AND SERVE AS A SQUADRON COMMANDER OF A COMBAT AVIATION SQUADRON.

services on equal footing with men. The navy
had broken the sex barrier by swearing in six
women pilots as naval aviators in 1974, and the
air force had followed suit in 1976. But women
were allowed to fly only in noncombat situations.
Beginning in 1993, women were allowed to fly
in combat.

- In 1993, it recommended that women be
  integrated into all military ceremonial units, such
  as ceremonial guard units and the Army Drill
  Team. It also recommended that Pathfinder
  training be open to women as well as men.
  Pathfinders guide paratroopers (airborne soldiers)
  to parachute drop zones.
- In 1996, it recommended that the navy open to
  women all types of ships and vessels.
- In 1999, it recommended that women be
  allowed into the Special Operations Forces
  (those involved in scouting, special operations,
  and counterterrorism). Today, women are serving
  in the U.S. Special Forces Command.

DISCRIMINATION IN THE MILITARY

By choosing to enter what has traditionally been a male-
dominated field, women are likely to encounter many men
who perceive them as weaker and who question how they
will hold up under the stress of military life. This is a particular
concern for women who are sent into combat areas. Even
though the U.S. military does not place women in direct
combat, their support positions often bring them into danger,

♀ SEXUAL HARASSMENT SCANDAL IN THE MILITARY

In September 1991, during a convention held in Las Vegas, Nevada, by the Tailhook Association, eighty-three women said that they had been victims of sexual assault and harassment. The Tailhook Association, which gets its name from the hook that catches the tail beneath an aircraft and a wire on the flight deck of an aircraft carrier, is a private association for active duty and retired navy and marine aviators who come together annually for a meeting on aviation issues. On one night of the convention, some partying got out of hand. A number of active duty female navy personnel were reportedly sexually assaulted. This led to a long investigation of allegations made by the women as well as a number of lawsuits. Despite the actions of the investigators and prosecutors, not one of the 140 cases ever went to trial. However, sometime later, the fallout from the Tailhook scandal continued, and the careers of 14 admirals and about 300 aviators were damaged. The failure to punish the offenders severely, though, reflected the gender issues faced by the navy as women decided to serve in that branch of the military. The Department of Defense has instituted new sexual harassment polices, in addition to programs for reporting harassment and assault anonymously. Some writers and journalists believe that the Tailhook scandal emphasized the changing status of women in the military, especially their role in combat.

especially when serving in areas like Iraq and Afghanistan, where enemy combatants may be anywhere.

Many men in the military come from traditional house holds where the men do physical labor and the women take care of the home and children. Such men may have difficultly accepting a woman as capable of being a soldier in the same way that a man is. In the military, people's lives may depend on the behavior and responses of their colleagues. Men may see a woman as likely to break under the emotional stress of combat and thus put their lives in danger. Others may see women as causing men to act less tough and aggressive—behaviors they see as part of the warrior creed, as well as critical to maintaining their fighting edge.

Such attitudes led to some major incidents when women first began entering the military in significant numbers. Women have historically faced the most resistance to their

A FEMALE FLIGHT SURGEON IN THE U.S. NAVY PROVIDES NECESSARY MEDICAL TREATMENT AND TRAINS LOCAL FEMALE MEDICAL STAFF AT A WOMEN'S CLINIC IN AFGHANISTAN. MALE MEDICAL PERSONNEL CANNOT DO SO BECAUSE OF CULTURAL TABOOS.

presence in the Marine Corps, a service whose male participants have long viewed themselves as elite warriors. In 1991, the Women's Services Integration Act recommended that the Marine Corps address policies that keep women from being fully accepted in the marines. Recommendations included the removal of gender-specific labels such as "women marines," elimination of differences in training, and an increase in the number of female instructors used to train male recruits. They also suggested eliminating the slogan "A Few Good Men" from marine recruitment campaigns.

DISCRIMINATION AT MILITARY ACADEMIES

Women have faced serious discrimination in major military colleges and academies, both in getting admitted and in the treatment that they receive after they arrive. The Military College of South Carolina, better known as the Citadel, is one of six military colleges around the United States. It provides military-style training as well as academic courses, and roughly 30 percent of its graduates enter the armed forces. It became notorious in 1995 when a female applicant, Shannon Faulkner, who was denied admission, engaged in a lawsuit against the institution. Faulkner won her suit and entered the college. A week later, she quit. She cited psychological abuse, among other reasons. The Citadel dropped its all-male policy shortly thereafter, however, because the U.S. Supreme Court ruled against the Virginia Military Institute, which likewise had an all-male policy. Four women were admitted, but trouble continued. In 1996, the Citadel suspended a cadet and relieved five others of their commands because of the harassment of female cadets. In 1999, Nancy Mace became the first woman to graduate from the Citadel. Yet a 2006 study revealed that harassment continues to be a problem for women, with nearly 20 percent of the female cadets reporting that they have been assaulted. Half of the women said that they didn't report incidents for fear of being further harassed. Sixty-eight percent of the women reported one or more incidents of sexual harassment, including sexual stories, jokes, and offensive remarks.

Similar problems have occurred at academies charged with training officers for U.S. military services. Despite the fact that the Air Force Academy has been admitting women since 1976, it has had repeated problems. In 2003, a sexual assault scandal erupted at the Air Force Academy in Colorado Springs, Colorado, which led to the firing of the academy's leadership. Nearly 150 women claimed to have been abused there between 1993 and 2003. Despite the fact that the situation led to a review of the military's policy on sexual assault, a 2005 survey of cadets revealed that 22 percent of male cadets did not believe that women belonged at the academy.

The U.S. Military Academy at West Point, which trains U.S. Army officers, has experienced similar problems with sexual harassment. About 15 percent of the academy's four thousand cadets are women. A survey revealed that about 10 percent of the female cadets reported incidents of sexual harassment. West Point began admitting women in 1976. In 1990, Kristin Baker became the first female First Captain, the cadet brigade commander at West Point.

The appointment is given to the student deemed to excel in athletic, academic, and leadership abilities. The First Captain is essentially the boss of all cadets. Not everyone thought this was a positive step. Not only were some male cadets resistant to taking orders from a woman, but the academy also received a slew of letters from West Point alumni objecting to the appointment of a woman as First Captain.

In May 1999, Nancy Mace, the first female graduate of the Citadel, receives her diploma from her father, Brigadier General James Mace, who also graduated from the Citadel.

In response to the problems experienced by female cadets, the House Armed Services Committee of the U.S. Congress created a task force in 2004 to investigate the issue at the air force, military, and naval academies. All the academies have instituted zero-tolerance policies for sexual abuse, and West Point now provides special advocates and counselors for women who experience sexual abuse.

CHAPTER 8

FUTURE TRENDS

In the last twenty-five years, progress has been made in attaining better treatment for women in the workplace. However, in many cases, there is still a gap between the ways that women and men are treated. Some of these differences are the result of lingering cultural attitudes that must be changed. Some require women themselves to stand up for their rights. Some require additional legislation and the strengthening of the federal agencies that enforce such legislation. Several factors are likely to affect the continued progress of women in the workplace.

WOMEN, WORK, AND THE FUTURE

The U.S. Department of Labor predicts that by 2016, 49 percent of the workforce will be female. The fastest-growing fields will be physical health care and social and mental health care, and these fields will continue to be dominated by women. However, if women want to make real progress in the workplace, they will need to expand their presence into other fast-growing scientific and high-technology fields that are presently dominated by men, such as engineering and information technology (computer hardware, software, and services), veterinary medicine, personal financial advice, forensic science technology, and environmental science.

One issue affecting the growth of the number of women in the workforce is the state of the economy. After the housing and stock market crashes of 2008, the economy took a serious downturn. As sales fell, businesses started laying off employees, and unemployment began to rise. Women are particularly vulnerable in economic downturns. First, they are more likely to be employed in part-time positions, which are often the first jobs cut. Second, in positions where seniority is an issue, the fact that women have been hired in large numbers only recently means they are likely to have less seniority and thus be laid off before men who have been in their positions longer. In addition, companies are more willing to invest in non-core business activities, such as human resources initiatives, when the economy is good and they are making a lot of money. During economic downturns, companies focus on reducing costs. As a result, they often cut back on staff and programs in areas like human resources. Or they employ staff on issues such as coping with layoffs, rather than on improving the lot of workers.

WITH THE BABY BOOM GENERATION AGING AND PEOPLE LIVING LONGER, MENTAL AND PHYSICAL HEALTH CARE ARE LIKELY TO BE AMONG THE FASTEST-GROWING INDUSTRIES IN THE NEXT DECADE.

WOMEN-OWNED BUSINESSES

Many women in recent years have started their own businesses. There are many reasons for this, but one is the feeling that they have reached the limit to which their present employer will promote them. The nature of women-owned businesses reveals much about the nature of women in the workplace in general.

Women starting their own businesses is the fastest-growing economic trend in the United States. This in itself reflects both women's desire to expand their opportunities beyond what is offered in their present job and the frustration that many feel at the limited opportunities available. According to the Center for Women's Business Research, 40 percent of all businesses in 2008 were at least 50 percent owned by women, compared to 30 percent in 2006. This supports a clear trend for many women to address the issue of inequality in the workplace by creating their own workplace. The number of women owned businesses has grown 46 percent from 1940 to 2006, twice the rate at which the number of businesses as a whole has grown. Women owned 20 percent of businesses worth $1 million or more in 2008. However, these businesses represent only 3 percent of the 10.1 million total women-owned businesses in the United States. And twice as many male-owned businesses have reached the $1 million mark.

One aspect of women-owned businesses may surprise you. Although one might think that these businesses are primarily started by college-educated women, one-third

♀ THE COLOR LINE

Women are not a single group, all of whom are the same. Women's prospects for achieving equality with men in the workplace can be influenced by factors other than gender. In the week preceding the 2008 U.S. presidential election, Princeton Research Associates conducted a survey for YWCA USA on the concerns of women from ages eighteen to seventy. They found a significant difference between the concerns of white women and those of black women in regard to workplace issues. When researchers asked subjects if they feared that certain factors would be obstacles to their progress in the workplace over the coming decade, they received the following responses from African American women and white women, respectively:

- Major illness or medical expense (84 percent vs. 68 percent)
- Unequal pay (81 percent vs. 55 percent)
- Affordable and accessible child care (72 percent vs. 57 percent)
- Limited opportunities for job promotion and advancement (72 percent vs. 41 percent)
- Lack of job-training opportunities (66 percent vs. 37 percent)
- Student loan indebtedness (62 percent vs. 33 percent)

These results support the idea that white women have a more optimistic view of their present and future position in the workplace than black women do, especially given that almost 60 percent of white women did not think that their opportunity for promotion or advancement would be limited, whereas 72 percent of black women did.

of women who start their own businesses have high school but not college degrees. Another clear trend is that the percentage of businesses owned by minority women is rising faster than any other segment. In 2008, minority women (Asian Americans, African Americans, and Hispanics) owned 26 percent of women-owned businesses. It is true that the economic downturn of 2008 is likely to affect both women-owned businesses and male-owned businesses. On one hand, it is likely to result in decreased business in many cases. On the other hand, because many women will find themselves laid off by their present employers as a result of cutbacks, more female-owned businesses may be started. One thing is clear, though, as Americans move through the twenty-first century: it is likely that the trend to open businesses will continue, and at least some $1 million-plus women-owned businesses started in the past few years will continue to grow and become more influential in the marketplace.

FUTURE TECH

One aspect of modern life that is improving women's earning power in the marketplace is technology. The discrepancy between men's and women's pay is greatest at the extremes of the work spectrum—in unskilled and semiskilled jobs, and in senior management, where women have had great difficulties breaking through the glass ceiling. In professional, technical, and middle-management positions, however, women have made significant strides. In such positions, technological skill rather than brute strength is often the determiner of success, and pay scales

in such areas are likely to be closer for men and women. In addition, obtaining the highest pay in such areas depends more on factors under the control of women: choice of work environment and skill in negotiating. For example, a doctor in a private group practice is likely to make more money than one working for a health

THIS WOMAN OWNS A CONSTRUCTION COMPANY IN ANCHORAGE, ALASKA. HER CONSTRUCTION BUSINESS IS JUST ONE IN A WIDE VARIETY OF BUSINESSES STARTED BY WOMEN.

maintenance organization (HMO). But she will have to assume more risk if the business fails, and she'll probably have to work longer hours. Thus, there is a trade-off between earning the maximum amount of money and having security, and it is up to the individual woman to decide where she is most comfortable. There is often a

tacit assumption that women should want to maximize their income at the expense of other aspects of their lives, but this is not necessarily the best decision for everyone—male or female.

The percentage of adult women in the workplace reached a peak of around 77 percent in the early 2000s. Since then, it has declined slightly to 75 percent. This

These students are participating in a program to encourage female students to become interested in careers in science. Today, women have opportunities for careers in a greater number of fields than ever before.

compares with 90 percent for men. However, the real question is not how many women are in the workforce, but whether they will someday have the same opportunities as men for high-paying, higher-status jobs.

CEO Chief executive officer; the highest-ranking manager in a company.

Civil Rights Act of 1964 Legislation that made it illegal to discriminate on the basis of race or gender.

depression A downturn in the economy.

dexterity Fine hand control.

docile Ready to accept control or instruction; submissive, or passive.

EEOC Equal Employment Opportunity Commission; the federal organization that deals with issues related to workplace discrimination.

fob off To put off with an excuse.

Fortune 500 A list of the five hundred largest companies in the United States, compiled annually by the business magazine *Fortune.*

FY Abbreviation for "fiscal year"; an accounting period of twelve months.

information technology The field of computer hardware, software, and services.

middle management Managers responsible for directly supervising employees or managing specific day-to-day functions of a company.

plaintiff A person who brings a lawsuit against a company or another person.

preconception An assumption formed before examining the facts.

predominant Major or primary.

preindustrial Describing the time when most goods were made by hand, rather than by machine.

prohibit To forbid.

prosperous Being comfortable and well-off.

retail trade The area of business in which items are sold to people.

segregation The action of setting someone or something apart from other people or things; an enforced separation of different groups in a country, community, or establishment.

senior management The highest level of management in a business, usually vice presidents and chief executive, operating, and financial officers.

Supreme Court The highest court in the United States; it decides whether or not rulings by lower courts comply with the U.S. Constitution.

sweatshop A factory or workshop where employees are forced to work in terrible conditions.

tacit Understood without being stated.

textile mill A factory that makes cloth from thread or yarn.

women's movement The organized effort by women to change the way they are perceived and treated.

Equal Rights Advocates
1663 Mission Street, Suite 250
San Francisco, CA 94103
(415) 621-0672
Web site: http://www.equalrights.org
This organization focuses on equal rights and economic opportunity for women and
girls. It provides counseling and legal assistance, as well as publications.

National Organization for Women (NOW)
1100 H Street, #300
Washington, DC 20005
(202) 331-0066
Web site: http://www.now.org
The National Organization for Women, started in the 1960s, is the premiere
organization working to promote women's rights. Its Web site provides a list of
local chapters and news on women's issues.

9to5
207 East Buffalo Street, #211
Milwaukee, WI 53202
(414) 274-0925
Web site: http://www.9to5.org
This organization is focused on bettering the lot of and winning equal treatment for
working women, especially those working in low-paying, traditional female
occupations.

Office of Women's Business Ownership Entrepreneurial Development

U.S. Small Business Administration
409 Third Street SW
Washington, DC 20416
(202) 205-6673
Web site: http://www.sba.gov

This office helps to establish and oversee a network of women's business centers and provides technical assistance to women who are economically or socially disadvantaged.

U.S. Department of Labor

Women's Bureau, Frances Perkins Building
200 Constitution Avenue NW
Washington, DC 20210
(800) 827-5335
Web site: http://www.dol.gov/wb

The Department of Labor provides information for women and reports on a wide range of topics relating to women in the workplace.

U.S. Equal Employment Opportunity Commission (EEOC)

131 M Street NE
Washington, DC 20507
(202) 663-4900
Web site: http://www.eeoc.gov

The EEOC assists women filing claims for discrimination. Its Web site provides detailed information on women's rights in the workplace.

Women Work!
1625 K Street NW, Suite 300
Washington, DC 20006
(800) 235-2732; (202) 467-6346
Web site: http://www.womenwork.org
This is a nonprofit organization that seeks to help women obtain jobs and improve their position in the workplace. It provides a variety of printed and online resources.

Workplace Fairness
2031 Florida Avenue NW, Suite 500
Washington, DC 20009
(202) 243-7660
Web site: http://www.workplacefairness.org
Workplace Fairness is an organization that provides resources for working people. It releases an electronic newsletter, information on court decisions, and information on attorneys.

WEB SITES

Due to the changing nature of Internet links, Rosen Publishing has developed an online list of Web sites related to the subject of this book. This site is updated regularly. Please use this link to access this list:

http://www.rosenlinks.com/wom/work

Bolles, Richard Nelson, Carol Christen, and Jean M. Blomquist. *What Color Is Your Parachute for Teens—Discovering Yourself, Defining Your Future.* Berkeley, CA: Ten Speed Press, 2006.

Busse, Richard C. *Your Rights at Work.* Madison, CT: Sphinx Press, 2004

Ehrenreich, Barbara. *Nickel and Dimed: On (Not) Getting By in America.* New York, NY: Holt, 2008.

Gourley, Catherine. *Gibson Girls and Suffragists: Perceptions of Women from 1900 to 1918.* Minneapolis, MN: Twenty-First Century Books, 2007.

Gourley, Catherine. *Gidgets and Women Warriors: Perceptions of Women in the 1950s and 1960s.* Minneapolis, MN: Twenty-First Century Books, 2007.

Gourley, Catherine. *Rosie and Mrs. America: Perceptions of Women in the 1930s and 1940s.* Minneapolis, MN: Twenty-First Century Books, 2007.

Howard, Linda Gordon. *The Sexual Harassment Handbook.* Franklin Lakes, NJ: Career Press, 2007.

Kessler-Harris, Alice. *Out to Work: A History of Wage-Earning in the United States.* New York, NY: Oxford University Press, 2003.

Seligson, Hannah. *New Girl on the Job: Advice from the Trenches.* New York, NY: Kensington, 2007.

Slomka, Beverly F. *Teens and the Job Game: Prepare Today—Win It Tomorrow.* Bloomington, IN: iUniverse, 2007.

Baxandall, Rosalyn, Lynda Gordon, and Susan Reverby. *America's Working Women: A Documentary History 1600 to the Present.* New York, NY: Random House, 1976.

Bonné, Jon. "A Gender Split in the Executive Suite." MSNBC.com, August 11, 2004. Retrieved January 6, 2009 (http://www.msnbc.msn.com/id/5624773).

Canada Department of Human Resource Development. "Gender Composition and Wages: Why Is Canada Different from the United States?" March 2000. Retrieved January 24, 2009 (http://www.hrsdc. gc.ca/eng/cs/sp/hrsd/prc/publications/ research/2000-000181/page00.shtml).

Equal Employment Opportunity Commission. "Filing a Charge." Retrieved January 12, 2009 (http://www. eeoc.gov/facts/howtofil.html).

Equal Employment Opportunity Commission. "Sexual Harassment." Retrieved January 12, 2009 (http:// www.eeoc.gov/facts/fs-sex.html).

Farrell, Warren. *Why Men Earn More.* New York, NY: American Management Association, 2005.

Grant Thornton. "Four in Ten Businesses Worldwide Have No Women in Senior Management." 2007. Retrieved January 5, 2009 (http://www. grantthorntonibos.com/Press-room/2007/ women-in-senior-management.asp).

Kaufman, Gil. "Many Female Cadets at Citadel Reporting Sexual Assault." MTV, August 26, 2006. Retrieved January 5, 2009 (http://www.mtv.com/news/articles/1539311/20060824/story.jhtml).

Lyness, Karen S., and Madeline E. Heilman. "When Fit Is Fundamental: Performance Evaluations and Promotions of Upper-Level Female and Male Managers." *Journal of Applied Psychology*, Vol. 91, No. 4, 2006, pp. 777–785. Retrieved January 12, 2009 (http://www.uwindsor.ca/users/t/tsirois/GradAppl.nsf/9d0190//a3c4f6768525698a00593654/6c9e6979hhh?5cuc85256e1d006734ca/$FILE/Lyness_2006.pdf).

MSNBC.com. "Working Women Do More Chores Than Men." September 14, 2004. Retrieved January 12, 2009 (http://www.msnbc.msn.com/id/6011245).

New York Times. "Citadel Suspends Second Cadet in the Inquiry on Hazing Women." December 18, 1996. Retrieved January 6, 2009 (http://query.nytimes.com/gst/fullpage.html?res=9D02E6DB1F3EF93BA25751C1A960958260&partner=rssnyt&emc=rss).

Pear, Robert. "House Passes 2 Measures on Job Bias." *New York Times*, January 10, 2009, p. A13.

PR Newswire. "YWCA Survey Shows Greater Economic Concerns Among Black Women Than White Women." January 2009. Retrieved January 12, 2009 (http://

findarticles.com/p/articles/mi_m4PRN/is_2009_
Jan_13/ai_n31188076).

Repa, Barbara Kate. *Your Rights in the Workplace.*
Berkeley, CA: Nolo, 2007.

Spraggins, Renee. "Current Population Reports: Men and
Women in the U.S." March 2002. U.S. Department of
Commerce, Census Bureau. Retrieved January 10,
2009 (http://www.census.gov/prod/2003pubs/
p20-544.pdf).

Sutherland, Daniel E. *The Expansion of Everyday Life
1860–1876.* New York, NY: Harper, 1990.

U.S. Department of Labor. "10 Top Jobs for Women."
2007. Retrieved January 12, 2009 (http://www.dol.
gov/wb/factsheets/20lead2007.htm).

U.S. Department of Labor Bureau of Labor Statistics.
"Highlights of Women's Earnings in 2007." October
2008. Retrieved January 12, 2009 (http://www.bls.
gov/cps/cpswom2007.pdf).

U.S. Department of Labor Women's Bureau. "Employment
Status of Women and Men in 2007." May 13, 2009.
Retrieved January 7, 2009 (http://www.dol.gov/wb/
factsheets/Qf-ESWM07.htm).

ABOUT THE AUTHOR

Jeri Freedman earned a BA degree from Harvard University. For fifteen years, she worked in administrative and managerial positions in high-technology companies. Among her responsibilities were running employee training programs and creating audiovisual training materials. Among the previous books she has written for young adults are *Privacy vs. Security* and *Cyber Citizenship: Intellectual Property*.

PHOTO CREDITS

Cover © www.istockphoto.com/Jacob Wackerhausen; pp. 6–7 © www.istockphoto.com/Chris Schmidt; pp. 10–11, 17, 30–31 © Bellmann/Corbis; pp. 13, 20 Library of Congress Prints and Photographs Division; pp. 22–23 © John Springer Collection/Corbis; p. 25 © Najiah Feanny/Saba/Corbis; pp. 28–29 © Roger-Viollet/ The Image Works; p. 36 © www.istockphoto.com/James Courtney; pp. 38–39 © www.istockphoto.com/morganl; p. 42 © www. istockphoto.com/Jeffrey Smith; pp. 44–45 Dennis Galante/Corbis; pp. 48 krtphotos/Newscom; p. 53 © Jack Hohman/UPI/Landov; p. 57 Brian Prechtel/USDA; pp. 58–59 © Jim West/The Image Works; pp. 60–61 © www.istockphoto.com/Oktay Ortakcioglu; pp. 65, 88–89, 96–97 © AP Images; p. 69 Karen Moskowitz/Taxi/Getty Images; pp. 70–71 Mark Wilson/Getty Images; pp. 74–75 © Sven Hagolani/zefa/Corbis; p. 77 © www.istockphoto.com/Peter Finnie; p. 82 U.S. Air Force; p. 85 Lance Cpl Diana M. Speicher/U.S. Marines; p. 92 © LWA-Stephen Weistead/Corbis; pp. 98–99 DOE.

Designer: Nicole Russo; Editor: Kathy Kuhtz Campbell; Photo Researcher: Amy Feinberg